WELCOME TO WOMANHOOD:

A Pre-Teen Survival Guide

Dr. Ciara L. Bostick
©2016

About The Author

Dr. Ciara L. Bostick has proven herself as a motivational speaker, college professor, and notable leadership trainer. In 2009, Dr. Ciara established a nonprofit organization, God's Gift, Inc., whose mission is providing a healthy environment for girls ages 7-17, by offering mentoring programs, weekend retreats, career development and training, college preparation, and most importantly helping girls to recognize their self-worth. God's Gift, Inc. caters to girls throughout disadvantaged areas in Broward County, Florida. Over the years, Dr. Ciara has partnered with many churches, schools, and community centers to encourage young girls worldwide with the message of self-worth.

Table of Contents

Chapter Four
Let's take care of that body!

Your crowning glory
What should I wear today?
Two Ears: All hearing
Don't forget those pearly whites
Welcome to womanhood!

Acknowledgements

"All my life I have worked with youth. I
have begged for them and fought for them
and lived for them and in them. My story is
their story."
-Mary McLeod Bethune

First and foremost, to God be the Glory for
the miraculous journey that he has set out
before me. Without God, nothing would be
possible. To my parents, Russell and
Andrea, thank you for your support and
prayers that have traveled with me
throughout the years. To the staff of God's
Gift, Inc., Ms. Barbara, and those near and
far, thank you for believing in my dreams
and supporting my vision. Your support
does not go unnoticed and has been a great
blessing throughout this journey. This is
only the beginning.

Introduction

I remember middle school like it was yesterday. I went from being the short, chubby little girl to the tall, skinny, bug-eyed girl overnight. I felt so awkward. All my friends looked totally different from me. They all had "features" I didn't have. All I had was a face full of bumps and thick reading glasses! So embarrassing! I didn't understand it. Why do I look so different? Things only got worse when my TIME came. Do I tell my mom? Do I tell my cousins? What's going on with me? These were all the questions going through my head. Becoming thirteen was the worse headache ever. I was literally freaked out, scared, and terrified, happy, excited...all of these emotions mixed up in one. Until I realized, I wasn't the only girl in school who felt awkward about having a period, and who was a random ball of emotions every 4 weeks. The older I got, the more comfortable I became with everything. Growing up isn't so bad, especially since our voices don't change like the boys! I realized that it was all a part of the process. I just wished I had someone older, like a big sister, to teach me all of these things.

That's where this book becomes in. The purpose of this book is not talk about all the gross things that happen during puberty, but to give you the ins and outs of what's expected and, how to deal with other issues that may arise, such as peer pressure, gossip, bullying, etc., as well other important topics for young girls to discuss like hygiene, clothing, serving, and praying. As your new BIG SISTER, I want you to be prepared for what's ahead, and I want to encourage you to fulfill all your hopes and dreams.

So grab a pen, notebook, and, highlighter and take notes. Let your big sis welcome you to womanhood!

1

Chapter One
What you SEE is WHAT you get!

You've heard it time and time again...self-esteem, self-esteem, blah, blah, blah...So what exactly is self-esteem? Well, [1]self-esteem's definition is "a feeling of satisfaction that someone has in himself or herself and his or her own abilities". "So, what exactly does this have to do with me?" PLENTY.

Most people have been taught that self-esteem has more to do with how you look, or whether or not you like yourself, but according to the dictionary it's really more about accomplishments. This is where all of Chapter Two of this book come into play.

When you do good works, it really does reflect on you, literally from the inside out. At this point, you have the basic stepping stones to building an awesome self-esteem. You know that the words that come out of your mouth affect the way you, and all the people who come into contact with you.

At this point, even your family will start to show you a new line of respect that you have never known before. You're growing up, taking responsibility for your actions and becoming a contributing person to society.

Guess what? If your parents are noticing, so will everyone else around you. Don't be scared. You have no fear because you're on

---

[1] "self-esteem" Webster Dictionary for Students. Merriam-Webster, 2011.

the right track to becoming a successful adult.

What if I'm not there yet? What if my self-esteem is low? If you have been following along with the book, and doing everything as described, you can't help but to have a better self-esteem.

Again … this has nothing to do with your self-respect. There are things that only deal with the world around you. It's how you react and act to those life changes that makes or breaks your self-esteem.

If you have the ability to change your goal in mid-goal then you're already golden. Most people don't shift gears so easily, even adults have this problem, but we'll go into more detail in the section titled Self-Respect. For now, just know that as long as you keep working on your goals, you will stay golden.

Don't be insensitive to the people around you. Ask how you can help. If it's a divorce, it's easy to feel like your insides are now on your outsides. It will make it difficult to keep doing life. DON'T let life's situations STOP you from keeping your self-esteem up.

Communication is always the key to a healthy relationship with anyone in your life. If life is rushing at you, it might be time to pray. Just don't give up. There's nothing so horrible in life that would make you give up.

Making me feel good through me

What does it mean? We already know that self-esteem deals with our actions then self-respect probably deals with how we feel about ourselves. The meaning of self-respect is [2]"someone's proper regard for himself or herself as a human being".

How much do you like yourself? We aren't going to talk about your body image here but it's important. It will be discussed in another section of this book.

How are you feeling about everything you do right now? At any moment it can change. It would be great if we could have high self-respect every moment of every day, but we don't. If you are lucky, you'll have it 99.9% of the time. It doesn't always work that way.

Did you fail to do something you knew was right because you were tired? Or having a bad day? Maybe you reacted and snapped at someone who irritated you. It happens. It happens to all of us at some point. No one is perfect. No one expects you to be perfect. This is where apologies enter in. You get a do-over.

It's also important for your self-respect to apologize the right way.

"How do you apologize the right way?"

---

[2] "self-respect" Webster Dictionary for Students. Merriam-Webster, 2011.

Most people say an apology by saying, "I'm sorry." This doesn't really cut it. At some point it gets shortened down to "sorry" in a flippant "I'm not really sorry" reply. It will at some point make you wonder about other people's apologies. It will make it easier for you to not be sincere the next time you apologize. Even more importantly, people will not trust or believe you when you do give an apology.

What does this have to do with self-respect?

When you apologize with all your heart and receive an apology in the same way, you never have to let yours or other people's emotions affect your self-respect. It's too easy to take others actions toward you personally. The reality is that their actions, or lack of actions, may only have 5 to 10 % to do with us. That is if the other person is a family member or loved one.

"So how do I apologize correctly?"

You start by saying, "I apologize for (whatever you feel you've done wrong). I didn't realize it would hurt you this much." This isn't just going to roll off your tongue. This will have to be learned and repeated over and over again just like saying "I accept your apology."

Don't say it unless you mean it. When we half-heartedly apologize, or accept an apology half-heartedly, we set ourselves up for disappointment.

There's more to an apology than giving it or accepting it. An apology means more than "I'm sorry I hurt your feelings." It means "I have to take a look at the behavior that hurt you. It's probably something I shouldn't do OR if I do have to do something similar, I'll have to do it with a different approach". It seems so simple but it isn't always.

Our actions often speak louder than our words. When we hurt someone else's feelings we have crossed a line. If we really want to be better, then we have to do something different. Give the apology and change the behavior. Accept the apology and let it go. Just do it.

Without self-respect and self-love you'll be lost. Have you ever heard the expression you have to love yourself for others to love you? It's true. Self-respect and high self-esteem equal self-love ... a whole person.

Disappointment leads to self-doubt. Constant self-doubt goes into low self-respect. At some point you emotionally shut down and lose self-respect. So how do you prevent low self-respect? You keep working on your self-esteem. They're kind of a couple. They start forming the minute you were born.

Who am I?

This is a question you will ask yourself more than once in your lifetime. Here's a little secret. Everyone in the world has asked themselves this very question at one time or another.

We didn't come with a book of instructions specifically for us. We are born into a world that for the most part we have no control of. The only thing we do have control of is our actions and reactions.

When we were little we take cues from the people around us. If they're "good" people, they will give us positive feedback when we do something right. If they're "bad" people, they will give us negative feedback.

The argument of nature versus nurture is a great one, but too much for where you're going right now. The bottom line is it's totally awesome that you're asking the question, who am I? It means that you're thinking about what you need to do to make yourself a better person.

So, ask yourself ... who am I?

Sit down and write down all the things you think makes *you* up. What does it all mean? If there are quite a few things on the page, it probably means you're a complicated person. Everyone is. So what do you want to do now that you see yourself on paper? Are you everything you thought? Less? Or more? Do you like what you see? (You will after you have been working yourself through the other chapters.) What would you like to do to make yourself a better person? Maybe run ... not walk to the next section: What's cool about me?

What's cool about me?

This is one of those questions that can drive you crazy. First of all, what is your definition of cool? The problem is your definition of what cool is today will change tomorrow, six months from now and even six years from now. There's no right or wrong definition because what's "cool" is constantly changing. What the world says is "cool" is not necessarily "cool" for you.

There was a time when all the "cool" teenagers smoked cigarettes. Ummm.... YUCK!, but true! It was sort of a rite of passage. Did it really make someone look cool? Not really. Why? Because it usually meant they were more worried about what their friends and peers thought (PEER pressure) than what they knew to be the right thing to do. Fast forward to 2016, PEER pressure is still alive and we witness it every day among people in your generation. For example: being pressured to steal, fight, or even skip class.

Here's another secret ... there are a lot of adults who are controlled by PEER pressure too. They worry about what makes them "cool". "Why would an adult worry about what others think about them?" It goes with knowing the difference between right and wrong. The job of an adult peer is to let another adult know that their behavior is either acceptable or not. It really isn't supposed to be about trying to look cool or be cool. Although if you watch much television you know that adults can easily fall under peer pressure too. This is where it's important to be strong in your own person. If you like you then you won't even be thinking about whether your peers are pushing you to do the wrong thing.

It's easy to fall to teenage peer pressure when you have teenage anxiety constantly filling you up. Luckily for you, you have good self-esteem and enough self-respect to know the difference between right and wrong, and positive and negative peer pressure.

Believe it or not, your parents were teenagers once. They do remember what it was like. You can ask them what was considered cool when they were teens. What did others try to pressure them to do? This will probably start a really cool communicating moment that you'll both appreciate. Parents, since the beginning of time, have tried to convince their teen that being "cool" is about just being you. It's about making good choices for you. It's all about looking at all sides of the situation, and not letting others pressure you. It's about being able to say no and really mean it.

This isn't always going to be easy, but just remember ... the more you do it, the easier it gets. You can still be "cool" and have fun. You can still find "cool" things about yourself. Another really cool thing is when you take a look around you'll find other teens with the same fears feeling the same pressures. That fear is that there's nothing cool about me, and I don't fit in. I don't have any friends. Everybody else is cooler than me.

BIG SISTER TIP: **I've never fit in! I knew I was always different. Once I realized that, possibilities became endless.**

You're not just cool, you're special!

These things aren't true, even if you don't have friends. Maybe you're shy. Some people have a hard time finding their place in the world and friends. Falling to peer pressure will never get you real friends. No matter what there are friends for everyone who's willing to be friends.

Of course, if you live hundreds of miles from civilization then you're correct about being alone. (Hopefully you have family with you.) Once you start accepting you for you, you already know what's cool about you. Maybe it's your smile or your hair or your eyes. It could even be singing or drawing. Guaranteed ... there's at least ONE thing about you that's way cool because you are you. No fears, no worries ... just go out there and be yourself, you are worth it.

What do I see in the mirror?

There are hundreds of books out that deal with teenage angst and negative body image. A body image doesn't have to be negative, but all girls from ages 9 to 99 have to deal with negative body image most, this section will start there.

There's no such thing as a cookie cutter body unless you're a Barbie doll or any other 10" or 11" plastic doll that you might identify with. (Monster High dolls, Bratz dolls, Disney dolls, etc.) Someone once determined that if these dolls were true to life, they would be close to six foot tall and weigh anywhere from 125 to 135 pounds. This is totally unrealistic. Why? Most girls and women don't get to be six feet tall and very few are that thin. Yes, there are some tall, thin girls and women. The chance of you being one of them is even thinner.

Most young women and older women are between 5'3" and 5'9". Their weights can also vary. That's why clothes come in different sizes, right? One size fits all rarely fits everyone.

At one time most girls and women weren't considered obese, but those numbers have changed in the last twenty or thirty years. We aren't even talking about that right now. This section is about that awkward time in your life when your body is still growing, and it hasn't reached full maturity. Most people gain weight BEFORE they gain height. (Boys are included in this one.) This isn't a hard and fast rule BUT if you watch babies grow to age five, you'll see this happening.

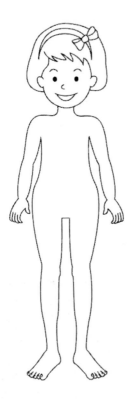

Why is it important here? If you feel like your ten pound weight gain is making you fat, it could just mean you're about to get a little taller. (If you gain ten pounds a week then it might be overeating or a metabolism problem.)

Whatever the reason, it's very important

to learn to LOVE the way you look. No, you don't have to look perfect. You just have to accept the way you look and your body.

We, as females, are taught to not accept our bodies. The awesomely funny thing about this is that the people who don't want us to love our bodies usually have problems with their own bodies. Regardless, anorexia and bulimia are still prominent with young girls to older women. (Yes, these two diseases don't stop just because a woman becomes old enough to know better.)

Ask yourself these questions. What do you see when you look in the mirror? Can you look at yourself in the mirror? (There are many who can't.) Do you try to eat all the right foods? Do you get some exercise every day?

Chances are if you're doing all the other things in this book, you're probably already trying to take care of yourself. It doesn't matter if you are tall or short, small, medium or even triple X large: the most important thing is to love and accept that this is your body. Once you do this, you'll be able to lovingly make any changes you think you need to make.

Just know that a five hundred calorie a day and ten thousand calorie a day diets don't work. If nothing else, this book is about finding a balance in your life. This includes your body image. You aren't going to love the way you look every moment of every day. What is important is that you realize that you can be the best you no matter what size you are.

If you aren't active, maybe you can find a way to include physical activity into your already busy schedule. Even walking around your house a few times a day can get your blood pumping. Blood rushing to your brain couldn't hurt your thinking.

BIG SISTER MOMENT:

Whenever you're feeling insecure, remember that short, chubby girl I wrote about in intro and how she became that tall skinny girl.

Love yourself regardless of how you look or how anything thinks you should look, you were created in God's image!

Chances are if you have a problem with your body image, someone has noticed. Not always. If you feel like you're too heavy, but others say no, don't be afraid to talk to someone about it. It's so easy to get caught in the trap of over controlling your weight. How does it even happen? Sometimes it feels like so many people are telling you what to do, when to do it ... basically controlling your life. For some people, their weight is the only thing they can control.

You can control more than just the food you take in and the exercise you do. You can control how you act and react to others and situations. Up to now, this book has mainly been about loving and accepting others but now you need to take time to look at your body image and say ... "No, I don't have a perfect body. No one does, but I do have the best body for me right now. I love me from the inside out." Love yourself and everyone else will follow.

Go-go-go set a goal!

Goal setting is a key to success. Why? Most people don't set a lot of goals and that's okay for them, but you obviously want more out of life. (That's why you're reading this book, right?)

This is where the day planner and calendar come in handy. Some people don't feel like they're accomplishing anything unless they see a product at the end of the hard work and sometimes the end of the day.

When you study hard, the outcome is great grades that could equal scholarships and getting into whatever college or university you choose, not to mention you get to graduate. When you cook, you produce a good meal, snack or dessert.

If you really work hard, you produce something more than just the good student ınd daughter, you produce a better you.

Goal setting can be as small as doing one random act of kindness a day to getting all A's. Your goals are only limited by you. What do you want to do with your life?

One way of really cementing your goal setting is to write them down. Don't forget to reward yourself when you have accomplished even the smallest of goals. It's probably not a good idea to reward yourself with food every time, but think of other things you would really love to have or do.

Maybe there's a movie you would like to see, or maybe a CD that you want to buy. Set a goal to do and the reward is one of the two examples I gave. Yes, it might seem a little silly at first, but learning how to achieve goals now will help you when you're older and have your hands full with work and family.

This is the other reason to WRITE down goals. It's easy to get caught up in LIFE and forget your goals. Then at the end of the day you look back at everything you've accomplished. It's easy to get discouraged when nothing has been done. It's easy to get discouraged especially when one goal-less day turns into another goal-less day into months and even years of goal-lessness (is it that even a word?!? .... Trust me it can happen in the blink of an eye.

I hear you ... "Not me, I'm always going to accomplish my goals! Good for you.

WARNING! WARNING AMBITIOUS GIRL!

Always, ALWAYS set goals BUT keep in mind to have a Plan B if everything doesn't go perfectly. Don't let failure determine your goals. Why? Because even if you have never had major failures in your life up to today, your life isn't over. It will happen at some point. When it does just know that your life isn't over.

Failure is just a part of life. Most people take failure as a personal attack. Don't take it like that. It's a great big learning experience. Failure doesn't care about you or any other person in the world. You don't have "good" luck or "bad" luck that causes failures or successes. There is no such thing as either, although, we often refer to them when dealing with our successes or failures.

The bottom line is your failures or successes are determined by the amount of work you're willing to put into your main project in life … YOU!

Success and failure are just words. Success isn't ONLY if you make millions and own a fancy car. It's when you work hard to achieve your goals that you will feel successful-like me and writing this book! At the end of the day, as you rest your head on the pillow, ask yourself, "Did I achieve a small goal today? Did I achieve a large goal? Did I help someone besides me today? Did I help me today?" If you can honestly say you feel good about your day then you'll sleep peacefully.

Just as you achieve goals, small and large, SET new ones. (Don't roll your eyes!) Life is all about setting goals and achieving them. It's all about the journey, not JUST the destination.

2

Chapter Two
Your Words Have Power

Miss Manners, if you please!

I know what you're thinking ... "Why do I need to learn about manners? I know manners, and besides it's not the 1950's or a hundred years ago. How I act is fine?"

Maybe how you act is fine and maybe it isn't. It never hurts to learn, and have manners that NEVER go out of date or STYLE. (In other words ... you'll thank me later.)

We all know that it's important to say please and thank you. If you already do this then you're off to a good start, but manners are more than just saying please and thank you to people you don't know well like teachers, friends, parents, adults you know from the community and strangers. The people we often lose our manners with are the ones who are most important in our lives: our parents, grandparents, and brothers and sisters.

I hear you again ... "Why do I have to be polite to my parents? Brothers and sisters? Stepbrothers and stepsisters?" (Especially brothers, sisters, stepbrothers and stepsisters ...) While you're still in your "pre-teen stage" this one will be the most difficult to master. Why? It's obvious to me and probably to you too. (Which is why you're asking me why? Did I at least make you smile?)

Okay, the bottom line ... because they

are the closest people to you besides your parents. I should probably have added stepparents in that group too. No, we don't get to choose any of them, but that doesn't make it right not to be polite. As you're growing up there will be a struggle for Mom and Dad's attention and finding your place in the family. That doesn't mean you have to be a bully to get it.

At first, it won't be easy to be polite because most of us don't grow up in the perfect family. I'm not telling you to let your siblings abuse you. Sometimes it's important to pick your battles.

You'll be surprised how your brothers and sisters, as well as your parents, will react to your new found manners. At first, they might be suspicious wondering what it is you want. After a while you will find that they will react differently to you. They may even change their attitude toward you. This can be a big help when you're talking to your parents.

You might even start doing something you used to do with them when you were younger ... you'll start communicating. You know ... share feelings; talk out problems with either Mom or Dad or maybe both. (Or even stepparents.)

I realize that a lot of teen girls and guys come from broken homes and blended families. This can work in these situations too. It will just take work BUT that is LIFE.

Life is work. Happiness isn't a pill in a bottle that we get to take once a day so we can deal with all of life's troubles. It's getting in there and living, and one way to make it easier is to have manners.

So what exactly are manners besides saying please and thank you? Let's break it down. We'll just touch on some things and go into more detail later in the book. Just keep reading.

1. Look people in the eye ... don't stare; it's not a staring contest. Make eye contact so that the person knows you're listening.

2. When you answer with a yes or no, don't nod or shake your head. No one can hear your brains rattle, silly. Speak up and say yes and no in a clear voice.

3. Say yes sir, no sir, yes ma'am and no ma'am. Some people claim this isn't necessary these days BUT it shows you have respect for yourself as well as the other person. People LOVE feeling like they're being respected. You know you like being treated with respect. So why not do the obvious? Treat others as you wish you were being treated. (This is so important it will probably be repeated more than once in this book. Be patient.)

4. Be patient with EVERYONE around

you.   EVERYONE.   Most importantly, you have to learn how to be patient with yourself.

5. Think before you do. This will be another difficult rule because we live in a world where people act without thinking. What does this have to do with manners? Let's spell it out in one easy word ... YOUTUBE. You never know when someone is making a video of you doing something embarrassing. This goes without saying, but DON'T pull out your phone and start recording everything in your life. Not every minute of your life should be broadcasted on YOUTUBE or any other social media. If you see someone who's having a difficult time or having a joke played on them, DON'T pull out your phone and start videoing. Don't post someone else's humiliation. It goes right back to what was said before ... DON'T do to someone else what you would not want done to you.

6. Be helpful. Look around you. There's always someone who could use a helping hand. (Especially Mom and Dad and this includes any stepparents and grandparents. Let's not forget brothers and sisters! More details about this in another chapter,

but for now ... just do the right thing.)

7. Clean up after yourself. No explanation necessary but ... there's no such thing as "That's not my mess." Trust me, your parents will already be noticing your changes if you follow these rules. You may even hear them say to your siblings, "I wish you could be more like _____." Don't get a big head. Just keep doing what you're doing.

8. Smile. Smile even when you're having a bad day. Smile even when the other person is having a bad day.

9. If you don't understand, ask a question. Don't be afraid to speak up. In fact it's always important to speak clearly. If someone doesn't understand and asks you to speak up or explain, answer them. Always be polite. Remember ... if you feel like you have a million things running through your head and a million things demanded of you ... they probably do too.

10. Remember ... if you start by being polite to you, you're going to be polite and use manners with everyone in your life. Life can only get better!

Everybody loves a compliment-I know I do! This starts from the time we're little and goes on until the day we die. Some of us seek out compliments. Who doesn't love a good compliment, especially when we're having a bad day?

Compliments are two parts to a Reese's candy. You have the peanut butter and the chocolate (YUM! …that sounds pretty good right about now!) Okay, seriously … compliments do have two parts.

1. We have to give them.
2. We have to get them.

Okay, stop laughing. It seems simple, right? Yes and no.

Sometimes when you look at someone and they have a really great outfit on, or maybe someone has written a paper that the teacher really likes we may find a little bit hard to compliment another girl or woman.

> **BIG SISTER TIP:**
> Women should also compliment one another. We are not in competition with anyone except the girl we were yesterday!

If you see another person working really hard on something, the compliment you give tells them that their hard work is paying off. Even if you never get another compliment in your life, it shouldn't keep you from giving them. NEVER give a compliment with the idea that the person should give you a compliment right back. Don't be greedy, be grateful. If you do get a compliment say thank you, but don't let it divert you from the compliment you're giving out.

Sometimes we females like to do that. Most of us don't know how to take a compliment either. Instead of the polite answer of "Thank you", we feel like we have to qualify it. Here's an example.

Kim: "Wow! That dress looks really great on you! You're looking so beautiful tonight."

Taylor: "Are you kidding? This old thing? I'm surprised I could even squeeze into this one."

That's not accepting a compliment. That's actually putting it down. Did you read thank you in any of that? Neither did I? Don't be a compliment killer!

Another big no-no ... "Wow! That dress looks really great on you tonight!" So it didn't look good all the other times she wore it? It doesn't seem important, but chances are she will remember. Just be careful.

Make compliments sweet and simple. When the person starts explaining just be patient. If they never say thank you, don't sweat it. Don't let it stop you from giving compliments either. Remember ... it isn't about you this time.

When someone gives you a compliment, smile and say thank you. You can even say something like ... "You just made my day, thank you." You don't need to talk about the hours spent on picking out the outfit, new makeup or hairstyle tricks you're trying ... just smile and say thank you."

Don't be afraid to give compliments to people you see on the streets, strangers. You never know when one kind word can say so much to a person you don't know.

You don't live in their heads, (Thank God!) and they don't live in yours. (Another smile of relief.) It doesn't mean you can't say something especially when you see them, and you find something wonderful about them in the two seconds you see them.

We live in a small world with the Internet, and it gets smaller every day, but there's no excuse for not noticing the people around you. Take a look around you. Who looks like they could use a good compliment? Who needs something positive to make their day? To change their lives.

DON'T forget Mom and Dad!

One more thing... take a look in the mirror and say, "You look good today." Once you stop laughing, say, "Thank you".

Now that didn't hurt, did it?

BUDDY VS BULLY

Wow! This is a big one, isn't it? Bullying.

Bullying has been around since the beginning of time, and now that everyone has a smart phone and Internet access, it has gotten way out of control.

Before the Internet or social media a person just had to make it through the school day, and most of the time the person might see their tormenter before school, at lunch, on the walk home and maybe if they were unlucky … on the playground at recess. Yes, in elementary school, that's where bullies ruled.

Today, bullies are everywhere, twenty-four/seven. It almost makes you wonder why their parents aren't noticing. How do they even have a normal day, but this isn't about the bully

STUPID, UGLY, LOSER

right now. Right now it's about the victim.

Bullies are pretty picky about the type of person they pick on. Most won't pick on a person they know will fight back. Usually, the person who's being bullied has a physical or mental difference. Maybe the person is just different. Whatever the bully's excuse, it rarely is a good one.

Maybe you're getting bullied. It happens to the best of us. Most people will have at least one person in our lives who will try to make our lives a HORROR story. It's what we do with it that can make or break the bullying situation. No one has to be a victim forever. Sometimes when you're a teenager everything seems forever. It isn't. In reality, it's only a blink of an eye. It won't last forever, but you will learn so much from. For instance, like how to build you up while one person is trying to tear you down, because as an adult there will be days when you'll feel like the whole world is trying to tear you apart-I know firsthand!

Now if the bullying is physical, STOP reading and run immediately to a parent or teacher. Tell anyone and everyone until they hear you. No one has the right to put their hands on you.

Don't believe them. They're using your own fear to keep you trapped. For one thing, by abusing you, they're already trying to kill you, even if it's just emotionally.

Tell EVERYONE. Obviously telling

other young people probably won't make it stop. Tell Mom and Dad. Tell teachers and if all else fails ... go to the police. Take your evidence to them. Just don't take the bullying.

"Okay, I'm not being bullied, but I know someone who is, what do I do?" If this person is your friend this is probably a no brainer, right? You get your friend some help. You help your friend in any way you can. That's what friends do, right?

Maybe you two can take self-defense classes together. There's some truth behind those Karate Kid movies. It serves two purposes: learning self-defense and building self-esteem, plus there's nothing like a girl who can kick butt. Just ask Laila Ali or Rhonda Rousey!

There's one thing no one in this day and age can probably avoid ... public humiliation. It happens. Something doesn't go right, and we get embarrassed. To add to the humiliation, someone made a video and put it on social media. Now there's a backlash of biting and hurtful comments circling the globe with our moment of humiliation. WELCOME to cyberbullying.

"How do I deal with it?" Obviously it's not going to be easy to ignore, but you can do it. It's a little harder to ignore ignorant text messages, but not impossible. Luckily, today even aggressive texts that threaten a person with bodily harm can be used in court.

The bottom line is no one has the right to make your life so miserable that you begin to wonder if life is worth it. Luckily for you, in this day and time, people listen when you say someone is bullying you. People will help you or a friend if you ask.

If it's a stranger being bullied, what can you do to help then? Please don't just stand there and do nothing. If you're reading this it's because you're trying to make yourself a better person.

Don't walk away. Treat them as you would want to be treated. How would you want to be helped?

But wait a minute! Let me ask you question.... Are you the bully? Sometimes it's easy to be a bully and not even realize what you're doing.

Do you make fun of someone to impress others? Do you make fun of someone because they're different? Do you see a bunch of people laughing and making fun of someone who has just been humiliated in public and follow along with the crowd?

It's easy to get into this mode. We see this happening around us twenty-four/seven. If it's not in person, then at the movies, on television and social media.

While the rest of the world is saying this type of behavior is okay, there are a lot of hurt souls that say no. The flip side of the coin is that you never know when it might be your turn. When will the crowd turn on you?

It's not easy to not follow the crowd. Standing out is dangerous, but it's so worth it. People may try to bully you because you refuse to participate in their bullying others. Don't let them change your mind. This is another key to building self-esteem.

Bullying or anti-bullying also goes for family members too. If you're beating up a brother, sister, stepbrother or stepsisters just because you can, STOP! Figure out the real reason you feel the need to torture them other than because they're there. Remember … some day you may need these people to have your back. Isn't it time you had theirs?

It won't be easy, but you can do it. Of course, the payoff is that at first they will think they're dying and the family didn't tell them. (Made you laugh!) Seriously, it's a part of the whole politeness and learning to love yourself as well as others.

Don't be a bully and don't be bullied. EVER!

Why are we mad?

Some days, conflict and conflict resolution will feel like a battle at the United Nations and Israel; your parents or other authoritative figures are Iran and no matter what you do … it's going to be wrong. You're just waiting to see if they'll drop the punishment bomb.

It doesn't have to be this way. Conflict resolution is a tool you will use your whole life.

No, I'm not telling you that you have to do everything your parents ask ... no questions asked. This doesn't even leave room for asking to go to a party, or the movies, or anything else. You have to speak to them in order to communicate your feelings or wishes. (Wishes equal what I want to do.)

Let's go back to the beginning ... sometimes the conflict is small. You're going to a big dance and you're trying to figure out what outfit to wear. You spend an hour going through your closet, and finally end up wearing the first or second thing you picked out. Yes, this is a very small conflict BUT it has all of the same emotions behind it that the big conflicts have-FEAR.

FEAR. A four letter word that pretty much controls everything and almost everyone.

It took so long to pick out the right outfit because of fear. Will the guy I like think I'm pretty in it? Will my friends think it's cool? What if the girls I don't like are jealous? What if they aren't? Have I worn this to a dance before? Probably a whole bunch of other thoughts similar to this will be going through your head. That's okay. Just don't let your fear control you.

You know what? In the big picture it won't really matter. Maybe you'll recall the outfit twenty years from now and maybe not. Chances are not BUT what will you remember is whether or not you had a good time. How so-and-so's eyes lit up. Maybe he asked you to dance or for a date.

That's the deal. Once the conflict is over, the details start to blend together.

Conflict resolution is all about lessening your fears as well as the others you're in conflict with. Conflict can make your heart pound, your pulse race, and maybe even make you want to vomit. This is the old "fight or flight" emotion they used to talk about in school all the time.

Guess what? It hasn't changed. The only thing that has changed is how we deal with it.

The first thing you need to do is to take a couple of deep breaths. That's it. Inhale softly and slowly through your nose, exhale softly and slowly through your mouth. You might need to do this more than once. As your head begins to clear, it will be easier to think about what you need to do next. Okay, now that you're thinking more clearly think about what's at the bottom of the conflict. In other words, what started it? Is it simple like you wanted toast for breakfast and baby brother took the last of the bread? In that case, you might have to be the bigger person and let it go. Have a yogurt, or whatever else you can find. If you can, pick up a loaf of bread after school so this doesn't happen again. (Your Mom and Dad will be showing you all sorts of respect when you do this.)

What if it's a huge conflict? First, calm yourself again with the controlled breathing. Explain to the other person what you are seeing and feeling. THEN listen to the other person's side. DON'T interrupt. Just listen. Don't think about your side as the other person is talking. You'll miss something. JUST LISTEN. HEAR THEM. Most people listen, but don't really hear. They are usually busy thinking about what to say next, and how to get what they want.

Conflict resolution is NEVER about getting your way. This is so important it needs to be said more than once. CONFLICT RESOLUTION IS NEVER ABOUT GETTING YOUR WAY. It's about finding the best possible solution to the problem. Some days it will feel like a win for you, and some days it will feel like a loss.

Just remember, no matter how strong your emotions are at the time you're feeling … the other person/people are going through the same thing. Sometimes emotions will run high. If you or the other person needs to back off and discuss it at a safer time … do it. No conflict can be solved when no one is listening. It just can't be done. Use that time to think from the other person's head.

Maybe little brother just learned how to use the toaster, and he thinks it's cool. No big deal, right? Maybe your parents need you to come in at 10:30 PM that night because the next day they want to surprise everyone with a family day the next day. Who knows?

One of the best gifts you can give yourself in conflict resolution is to look at the problem through someone else's eyes.

Okay, the problem isn't going away. You have taken two or three time outs, but both of you still get angry when you try to discuss it. It might be time to take the problem to a third person.

It's important that it is someone you and the other person both respect and is neutral. Although you might find that some people are going to be fair even if it's their daughter, BUT not always. The neutral party is just so another conflict won't start over the decision. (Hey! Even adults can't always do this so don't sweat it if it takes a few times to get it right.) Agree that whatever the third person decides you'll both be okay with it. DO IT!

It's easy to say you will and then change your mind. There are at least two people to forgive in a conflict: you and the other person.

What does forgiveness have to do with conflict resolution? Again, during a conflict your emotions are racing, and fear has you trapped. Even when a peaceful solution has been found, it's too easy to store that memory away and bring it out again when you and that person get into another conflict. By forgiving yourself and the other person, it really is resolving the conflict. It's done. You never have to think about that problem again. Remember the tools you used to get conflict resolution, but not the conflict. (This might be a good time to say a prayer of thankfulness that you haven't lost a friend. Friends are awesome and make such a difference in our lives.)

Did you hear about ...?

This is a tough one. Why? Because most people gossip and don't really know they're doing it while they're doing it. Why? Most people don't understand the definition of gossip.

"A person who repeats stories about other people" or "talk or rumors involving the personal lives of other people". [3]What does that all mean? ...girl, YOU'RE A GOSSIPER!

Basically if you don't hear it from the person it happened to, or saw it yourself, it's probably gossip.

There are two types of gossip: good and bad. Don't get caught up in the bad or the

---

[3] "gossip" Webster Dictionary for Students. Merriam-Webster, 2011.

juicy gossip! Spreading rumors about someone isn't just gossiping, but in some instances can be considered bullying.

Why?

Because when you spread negative gossip about another person there's a good chance you're going to hurt that person's feelings. What most PEOPLE (Adults are included in this because they often do this too.) don't realize is that if I spread gossip about another person, then I'm giving people the right to spread gossip about me. I don't know about you, but that doesn't sound good to me.

People like to talk, girls and women especially, but don't get too worried: boys and men gossip too.

So what's good gossip?

It's not the type of gossip you sit around and get popcorn and listen to your best friend chit and chat. Good gossip might be considered good if you're telling someone good news like your friend's mother had a baby. Bad gossip might be telling everyone that the girl you've been fighting with since elementary school is pregnant when she isn't. Yes, it happens. The bottom line is rumors and gossip hurt.

The old saying "sticks and stones may break my bones, but words could never hurt me" are wrong. True, we all have a choice on whether we let those hurtful words harm us, but sometimes even when we say it doesn't matter, it does.

As a teenager with hormones filling your brain and all sorts of new responsibilities hitting you in the face, you need a positive word. In fact, you need a lot of positive words. So what does this have to do with gossip?

As you're sitting with your friends, and you all are discussing everything that's going on in your lives it will be easy for someone to say, "Hey! You know what I heard about so-and-so?"

Of course everyone is going to say, "No, what?"

It's at this moment you have a choice. You can encourage them to continue, or you can change the subject. If you're really brave you can say something like, "Were you there? How do you know this?" And if you're exceptionally brave, you might suggest not talking about that person especially if you know what the other person is saying either isn't true, or just the other girl putting down whoever she's talking about.

Yes, I hear you. This tactic isn't going to win you any popularity contests. If you won't gossip, and you won't tolerate gossip, people's attitudes will change toward you. That's okay. I promise it will be okay. This is when you start to see who your true friends are. You may find that some of the people that put others down are actually bullies. They aren't really true friends.

Just know that it you're feeling awkward and sensitive then EVERY girl around you is feeling the same way. This includes all those girls you think have it so together. Chances are they're feeling as confused as you. How crazy is that?

So when you aren't listening to gossip or spreading gossip, what can you talk about? A LOT! Shoes, clothes, Chris Brown, Justin Beiber...did I say shoes?

Just remember ... you have a choice. Think about it this way (as you're about to say something about another person), and ask yourself this question: "If someone said this about me would it hurt my feelings? Would it hurt my future choices? Would it follow me into my future?"

If the answers are yes, don't say it out loud. Just remember that many times an innocent person has been put to death, or killed because of gossip. Always think before you speak....ALWAYS!

Good from the inside out

There's nothing like positive affirmations to build you up. You might not be at the stage where you're ready to do light daily meditations, attend an early morning yoga session, but you should begin incorporating positive motivation quotes in your head now.

It's definitely not easy to start a program of daily affirmations. It might even mean that you have to get up a few minutes earlier, or get off social media a few extra minutes earlier before bedtime. (If you choose to do affirmations before you go to sleep at night, it will help you get plenty of rest.)

Daily affirmations give a positive message and encouragement out of a sometimes dark and gloomy place. Although they aren't for everyone, at some point in your life you will find them very encouraging. We all need a little extra encouragement, don't we?

So what exactly does daily meditations or daily affirmations have to do with you?

Ok so what is an affirmation? It's "an act of saying or showing that something is true."[4]

So, how does that work for you? Have you ever seen a woman standing in front of a mirror telling herself she's beautiful? She might even make you giggle when she says something silly like "I love you." I bet I made you giggle just by putting that image in your head.

You're probably even thinking this person is full of herself. No, not really. Sure, some people who might do this might be stuck up! (Clutches pearls!) You might find

---

[4] "affirmation" Webster Dictionary for Students. Merriam-Webster, 2011.

that some have very low self-esteem, and they really don't love themselves.

Don't worry about them … look at you!

What do you like about you? There has to be something. We'll go into greater detail about this in another chapter, but for now, find one thing you like about you and then build from there.

Another way to deal with affirmations is to give others affirmations. I'm not just talking about compliments, I'm talking about watching others around you and finding something about them you like. Then, tell them about it. Don't do this expecting something in return! No, that's not the point of this exercise. It's funny but as you start to notice good things about other people around you, you'll start to see good things about yourself.

The old myth that you're the one half of somebody else is wrong. You can't be a part of a couple if you aren't whole. What does this have to do with affirmations? You can't be a part of a couple if you aren't a whole person. It starts with giving you affirmations and loving yourself.

Take a look around you. Pick out another woman you admire that seems to have it together, watch her. What makes her stand out to you? Does this person practice positive affirmations? Practice what they preach? If she does, she's the one to watch.

Affirmations confirm on the inside what

we want to project on the outside. It shows the rest of the world that although you aren't perfect, you can work hard to the best person you can be. Say it loud and proud, "I'm the best person I can be." Then be you!

I dare you to:

- **Take some sticky notes (Post It's), and write down positive thoughts on each one, and post them in your room and around your mirror**
- **Every day, read them believe them, and let them motivate you.**

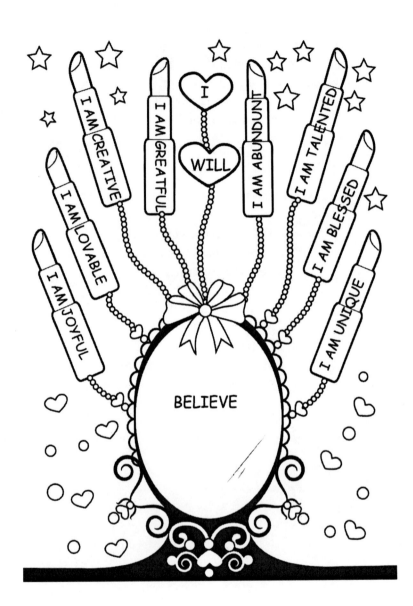

Dear God ...

Now this is something I eat, sleep, and live by...PRAYER! The moment you start a prayer you mentally and emotionally get out of yourself and whatever situation you're in, you take that five extra minutes to connect with something greater than you. Even if what you ask for is denied, at some point you have to look at the situation in a different light.

Praying is personal. It's probably as personal as it can get. Why? Because for the most part it's just you and God. Having a conversation that only you two can participate in.

Yes, there is public prayer and affirmations. Yes, there are prayers and praying that is done by family members, preachers and other community leaders. Praying is praying, even when we have those, "I haven't eaten all day, God please hurry before my stomach makes noise" moments. That's ok, a little different, but it's ok!

So what is praying all about? Yes, it's personal. Yes, it's something you can do at any time. You can even do it in a room full of people without anybody knowing as long as you don't get too loud.

So what does one pray for? What do you want to pray for? How do you pray?

Let's start with the last question first.

Everyone has their own idea of how to pray. Some will say you have to have a special place to pray. It's nice if you have it, but most people don't have this luxury.

Some people believe you need to get on your knees. Not going there. If you believe in dropping to your knees, no problem, but that isn't what this chapter is about.

It's about those moments when you aren't so comfortable in your praying. You've looked around you and you realize you might be doing it a little differently than others. That's okay too. We all have different personalities and life experiences. What works for others might not work for you, and what works for you might not work for others. You have to find what's comfortable for you.

Depending on your belief system, some religions say it's okay to pray for things. "Please, God, give me that brand new car for my sixteenth birthday." Did I make you giggle? If I didn't, that's okay.

No matter what most people believe there is one common theme for all whom pray … praying for those who are having a hard time or major traumas going on in their lives.

When we selflessly make the praying about another person, we get out of ourselves, and start looking at the people around us. We start appreciating what we do have even if it's just a cardboard box in the middle of a smelly, dirty alley. We aren't the center of the Universe when we're praying for others who have less ... that makes us better people every time. Begin writing your prayers in a journal and looking over them every day. You'll be surprised where a little faith can take you.

> **BIG SISTER TIP:**
>
> **Since I was eight, I've always had a journal. I wrote down my thoughts, hopes, and dreams.**
>
> **Try. You'll be surprised what manifest over the years!**

I'm so mad ...

OK, I know we just finished discussing how peaceful prayer can be, but let's be honest, we all get angry. Anger ... there's nothing that packs a punch into your stomach more than this six letter word. Why? Because it carries so much emotion behind it.

So what exactly is anger? Anger is "a strong feeling of displeasure or annoyance and often of active opposition to an insult, injury or injustice, to make strongly displeased, make angry[5]"

Now that you're a teenager-or almost a teenager, you may find that there are days when you will feel more irritated than usual. It will even at times feel like everyone is against you. They probably aren't. This is normal.

ALL young ladies and women go through this period at some point in their lives, but we'll talk more about this in the Hygiene: Menstrual Cycle section of Chapter Four.

What makes you angry? Every person has different triggers that can cause them to become angry. We, as humans, know what irritates our loved ones. Sometimes we might even do these things to irritate or anger our Mom, Dad, brother or sister. When we were little this could be great fun to bug a brother or sister whether they are older or younger. It's very normal. The problem comes when Mom and Dad have to step in to stop it. Not good. You know you're going to get into trouble, but sometimes it's so difficult to stop especially if brother or sister has done something mean to you.

Stop what you're doing. Take a look around you. At what's happening. Is there a good reason to be angry? If this happened six months from now would you still be

---

[5] "anger" Webster Dictionary for Students. Merriam-Webster, 2011.

angry? If the answers are no-then chill. Take a deep breath and think about why you're so angry. There are a lot of great reasons to be angry, but it's not about the anger that hurts so much as our reaction and actions to that anger that hurts us. Obviously, violence is never the answer unless you're defending yourselves. Why? Because it doesn't really stop the anger. It doesn't stop whatever made you angry in the first place from happening, but it might be able to stop it from happening in the future.

Lots of times anger comes from hurt feelings. Instead of telling the person everything that made you angry, you hold it inside and end up developing resentment. Resentments are never good. They're like a skinned knee on the inside. Every time something upsets you about this person or that person, you tear off the scab, make the wound bleed and at some point it becomes infected (graphic, I know...sorry!). In other words, it just doesn't work; it doesn't heal. You let your anger control you.

On the other hand, how often do you make another person angry? Do you find yourself fighting a lot with Mom and Dad? Brothers and sisters? Maybe even your best friend ... "No way! She's my best friend. I would never want to make my best friend mad at me."

It happens. All of it! There are just going to be times in your life (Everyone's life.)

where you try to find where you fit in. Plus, the only way to develop a more mature relationship is to change the way you speak with your parents and friends. The more mature level you speak with them, the easier your life will become.

Just remember ... someday you'll be a parent, and then you will understand what all those "unreasonable" requests your parents made meant. They love you. They just want to keep you safe. Despite what brothers and sisters say, they love you too. Luckily, even the worst sibling fighting will change as you become adults.

What about strangers? Is it right to do things just to anger people we don't know as well? Do you go out of your way to make them miserable? No, you shouldn't. It's always best to think back to, "How would I want to be treated?" If the answer is "Not like this," then don't do it.

Don't be a doormat BUT don't look for a fight either. Anger is never a solution to any of your problems. Anger is usually just fear turned inward, and dealing with it is the only way to be happy.

Respecting my elders

This can be a difficult one especially if you feel like the authoritative figures don't respect you. It's a game of tug-of-war that's probably been going on since the beginning of time, but maybe more so in the last hundred years. Why?

Well, within the last hundred years the child labor laws have changed. There was a time when many people don't go past third grade. They went to work instead. The work day was anywhere between ten and twelve hours a day and sometimes you worked seven days a week. (This is part of the reason most people didn't live as long as they do now.)

Who are the authoritative figures in your life? Why should you respect them? Authoritative figures are usually the people who have some sort of say about what's happening in your life. Unless you live ALONE in a bubble in the middle of the forest, desert, etc., there are going to be authoritative figures in your life. EVERYONE has at least one including your parents. They hold us accountable for our actions.

The first authoritative figures are our parents. Next comes all adult relatives, adult family friends, spiritual leaders, teachers, police, firemen, doctors, nurses, bosses and elderly adults ... did I leave anyone out? (You thought when you became an adult you didn't have to listen to anyone! You were wrong.)

Respect is the key to an awesome relationship. Going back to the dictionary, respect means, "high or special regard, thoughtfulness or consideration, to consider worthy of high regard".

Respectable. (I know that's not part of this chapter but maybe it is ... just listen.) Being "respectable" is simply being "decent or correct in conduct".[6]

I hear you already. "This is why I can't always respect _____ and _____. I know that _____ isn't living or doing the right thing." True, according to the definition you don't really have to give respect to people who don't live respectable lives. It doesn't and can't work that way for two reasons.

This session is about why you need to respect authoritative figures in your life. It's because of you. Respect, like love, is another one of those things that starts from the inside out. If you respect yourself it will be easier to respect everyone especially authoritative figures.

Parents are next on the list. No one asks them to be perfect. Fact is when you live with more people than just you, there has to be a level of respect for everyone in the house so it can peacefully co-exist BUT don't expect your parents to treat you like an adult unless you are one. For the most part, your parents are trying to teach you how to be an adult. They have years of experience

---

[6] "respect" Webster Dictionary for Students. Merriam-Webster, 2011.

dealing with life. They may not have been born with a cell phone in their hands or social media at their back, but they get the emotions that go with it.

Teachers and bosses are the hardest ones to respect. "They're always telling me what to do." That's true. It's their job. Your job is to do the assignments and turn them in. The grades are just an added bonus to let them and you know if you understood the lesson. When you go to work, you don't get that constant evaluating. Problem: sometimes they don't tell you when you have done it right all the time BUT they will always tell you when you did it wrong. (rolls eyes) When that happens, just shake it off. (The anger or the hurt ... don't shake off the instructions of how to correct your work. If they don't give any suggestions, this is the perfect time to ask questions. What should I do? How can I make my work better?) This can also be a great incentive to stay in school and go to college so you can get a better job.

Police are really here to help. It might not seem like it with all the things going on in the last ten, fifteen years. When a police officer stops and gives you a ticket, it isn't just to give you a fine or to cause problems with your insurance. It's to tell you that what you're doing might put you and others in danger. Granted not all laws are just, but we're just talking about respecting authoritative figures. Just smile and say thank you when the officer hands you the ticket. Better yet ... don't speed, text and always stop at the STOP sign.

Giving authoritative figures respect isn't always easy, but it shows more than you know ... it shows you respect yourself. You can't respect others if you don't start with you first.

3

Chapter Three
Get it HANDled!

Building me by building my community

I hear you ... "Isn't community service what you get when you get in trouble with the law?" Yes and no. Yes, people often do get community service when they get in trouble with the law. (Most people under the age of thirty probably think it's the only time one does community service unless they're on a college track.) No, you don't have to get into legal trouble to get community service. In fact it's probably easier to do community service when you aren't in legal trouble.

Why? Well, you have choices. Anytime you have choices, life is a little better.

Social service agencies, as well as the ASPCA and a few other organizations, LOVE young people who are just dying to do community service and BINGO! You're it.

Hopefully you live in an area where you have many, many choices. Some zoos actually have a program as well. If you are lucky you'll find a community program you love. (Just remember that whatever program you choose will look good on a college/university application. That's a plus for you.)

So where to start? Do your research. Find out which social service agencies are close to home. Here are some suggested places to look:

1. Soup kitchens or missions
2. ASPCA or animal shelter
3. Local Veterinarians
4. Local hospitals
5. United Way
6. Museums
7. Libraries
8. Zoos
9. Churches, synagogues and mosques

You probably won't be cleaning garbage off the streets or highways. Let's leave this community service job for the law breakers and those employed by the state.

What happens when you do community service? Two things:

1. The program you volunteer for gets some awesome unpaid labor that's so greatly appreciated in this time of tight budgets and government cutting back on social service budgets.
2. You get out of self and start to appreciate everything you have and even things you don't have.

For example: You might not like spaghetti Tuesdays, but at least you have food to eat. The person getting a meal at the soup kitchen may only get one meal a day. You know you're going home to a fully stocked kitchen. Volunteering gives you an awesome attitude of gratitude: Priceless!

Most people who do community service only do it once or twice a year, usually during the holidays when they feel the need to help out their fellow man, woman or child. It's easy to forget that people are hungry and homeless every day. Abandoned animals are a constant in our throwaway society. Older generations sit in nursing homes day after day, forgotten and alone with their thoughts. This happens every day: twenty-four/seven/365.

You can make their lives a lot easier. Sure, it might be scary at first, but what your visit to an older person might mean everything to them even if they never remember your name.

You might not want to volunteer at the animal shelter if your heart is too big. Why? Because your family might not be able to feed all the beautiful animals that you might want to bring home. On the other hand, if you really enjoy working with animals you'll find out if you can work with animals.

You may be worried that community service will take too much time. This is where making a schedule and keeping it helps. No one is asking you for all of your free time. Three or four hours a month will still count.

You may find that community service can turn into an awesome part-time job when you're ready. Animal shelters and veterinarians always need someone to come in on the weekends for the dogs' final walks and to clean up the accidents and kitty boxes. You make a face now, but you have to start somewhere. It might as well be doing something you like.

The golden benefit of doing community service is giving of yourself and feeling good inside because you've done a good deed. This can't be said enough. When you feel good about yourself on the inside, it'll show on the outside. Doing community service gets you out of yourself ... makes you a better person. (Plus it looks really great on job and college applications.)

Be a RASKAL Raccoon!

Random Acts of Kindness became popular back in the 1980s. It was developed by a woman named Anne Herbert in Sausalito, California. She even published a book titled "Random Acts of Kindness" [7]in February 1993.

Even back then there just wasn't enough kindness in the world. (Pre-everyone has a computer and Internet at home era.) People were doing for themselves and acting like they were the Sun, and the rest of the world was the Universe with it revolving around them. It's sad to say that nothing has changed. They didn't see the world around them, just themselves.

Fast forward until today ... today there is

---

[7] *Random Acts of Kindness*. Berkeley, CA: Conari Press, 1993. Print.

still a need for random acts of kindness. There's even a website, randomactsofkindness.org that gives you ideas for random acts of kindness. It also gives examples of random acts of kindness you can help them with, or you can start a chapter in your own community. You could probably make it your community service project if you wanted. There's a Random Act of Kindness week that takes place during February 14th-20th with Random Acts of Kindness Day taking place on February 17th. [8]But today let's talk about the true meaning of random acts of kindness that you can and should perform every day.

Maybe you have a younger brother or sister, you can take them to the park and let Mom and Dad have alone time. You could surprise the family by cooking dinner. It doesn't have to be a gourmet meal. Your family will appreciate anything you do if you do it with a kind and thoughtful.

There's more to the idea than meets the eye. Every day that you wake up and come into contact with others, you have the option to do a random act of kindness. Sometimes you just have to take a look around you … there's a woman in the store with a cart full of children trying to check out. All of the children are crying, distracting the mother and clerk. She'll be ever grateful if you talk

[8] "www.randomactsofkindness.org" 2016. Random Acts of Kindness

to the children, maybe calm them by just drawing their attention to something else.

An elderly person next door has a hard time getting around. Volunteer to help walk the dog or pick up her mail and newspaper.

Some acts of kindness really are random. You only have to take a look around you to see where you can help make this world a better place to live in. First, you have to get you out of you, see a theme here?

BIG SISTER TIP:

It's not a random act of kindness if you take pictures or selfies doing it and then flash them all over social media. These should be <u>selfless</u> acts of kindness.

In fact when random acts of kindness began, the idea was to see if you could do something wonderful without anyone knowing you did it. Yes, there were times when it's going to be obvious you did it but don't act like you did it to get something in return. Your goal is just to do something to help another. No reward necessary. People will thank you. Say "You're welcome," and walk away.

Everyone needs a little help at times in their lives. When we show even a sliver of kindness to another person, we prepare our hearts to receive kindness. It's all about making yourself a better person while you're helping the world.

Serving God

Every part of this chapter is about helping others, and this section is no different. This section deals with working with your religious community. Your church, synagogue or mosque, or whatever you deem as the center of your religious community.

Most have a youth group that you're probably already involved with. Your group may already be doing youth projects that involve the community and church. Great for you! You are already ahead of the game.

Serving your church community might be more than having a bake sale to help cover youth activities. What can you do to help the church? Your spiritual leader? Maybe it's something as simple as picking up the trash around the parking lot, the sanctuary and the bathrooms. Even if there's a full time janitor, s/he isn't there twenty-four/seven. Cleaning up after others helps you to acknowledge the times when you have left messes for other to clean up. No matter how good people are, they don't always think about picking up the trash.

You can even volunteer to rake up the leaves or cut the grass. Not all churches can afford a full time gardener.

When they ask for volunteers in the nursery, be one of the first to sign up. For some moms and dads, this is the only time they have a moment to breathe and worship without someone constantly tugging on their hands.

When services are over, be the one to help round up the children in the parking lot. It might seem like a little thing but on a busy street after church, it's priceless. You might even save a child's life.

But the kindness doesn't stop there. Maybe there are elders who just aren't physically able to get to services. There's nothing stopping you from going to their homes and sharing a prayer. Maybe you can take them a hot meal and share it with them. There's nothing like praying and sharing with an elder who has seen more than you, and can share some wisdom and history.

You never know when one of them will enlighten you with a story that will have you thanking God for all you have today. Plus, you'll be one more person checking on someone who doesn't always get a lot of company.

Don't forget your manners! There are other jobs as well like helping in the kitchen. Maybe you have awesome computer skills. If these are people you know, they would probably love to teach you skills like how to put together the weekly bulletin or monthly newsletter.

Serving isn't just about making sure everyone knows what you did it's about you doing something for the community because it's the right thing to do.

Helping hands to help others

Helping others has been covered in the other three sections to some degree, but what hasn't been covered is why you should do it.

You already know the difference between right and wrong. All of your life there are going to be times when you'll have to sit back and ask yourself, am I doing this for the right reason or the wrong reason?

If you're doing it because you truly want to help someone out of the goodness of your heart-that's the right reason. If you're doing it because you want others to like you, to get paid or just so others will think you're great-bad reason. Just remember, some day you will be old or need help. Wouldn't you want someone to help you?

Another big no-no … if you see something bad happening to someone don't just stand there and make a video. If you're the only one there, call 911, and then try to help the person. If you're with a group, have you or someone else call 911 while you and some of the others help that person. Unless the person has a gun, there's a chance that a group of people can easily scare off an attacker PLUS the closer you are the better the chance that you'll get a great description of the act and the person even if you have video. The act could have started even before you started videoing.

Don't just stand there. Do something. Video is great but it isn't great if you get a video and the person dies.

Helping others will make the smile on your face start in your heart and make you shine like a star, like says, "Just do it!" and help others every day.

4

Chapter Four
Let's take care of your body!

Your crowning glory

Hair is a woman's crowning glory. You've probably heard this before. It's true; even if you're of a religion that demands you cover your hair up or shave it off. Why else do we spend so much time and money on it?

Some hygiene issues with hair are obvious. How many times a week you wash your hair depends on your hair type. Thicker hair will probably not need to be washed every day. (You would be spending all your free time washing it.) Thinner, oilier hair types will need to be washed more often.

The important thing is to find what works for you. How long or short do you want your hair to be? "What sort of hairstyle am I going to wear today?" The great news is that no matter WHAT you do to your hair, it will grow back.

(Warning! Constant coloring your hair and some medications may change the thickness and type of hair you have, just BEWARE!)

If you go to a school that doesn't have a problem with you coloring your hair blue, go for it. (Be sure that your parents are okay with it too.) Hair grows out just make sure to do the basic maintenance with it every day like brush it, wash it when it's dirty and style it all you want.

FYI: Bugs can be in your hair! Even

the cleanest, richest person can get lice. Don't panic. If you're lucky enough to live in a large city there are places that you can go to and get treated. If you can do this, this will probably be your best choice because the chemicals in over the counter medication can be so harsh on hair. The salons that treat lice have gentler, friendlier methods.

If it's caught in time before the infestation gets severe, great. Some people go to drastic extremes such as cutting the hair short or off. You have to do what's best for you. Just remember, hair grows back. Don't share brushes or hats with the rest of the world. In other words, be very careful when you are hat shopping. This one is going to be tough. Just remember, if you want to try it on, others probably did too. BE CAREFUL! Treat as soon as you discover it.

Your hair is still your crowning glory. It tells a lot about you PLUS you can change it, all to your mood. If you have long, long hair and decide to do a short cut, DON'T forget those gorgeous locks of love!

What should I wear today?

You look in your closet and shake your head. "Ugh! I have nothing to wear." (Go ahead and laugh, you know you do it.) This is something ninety percent of your generation and all other women do every day. If you're lucky or unlucky, enough to go to a school that says you must wear a uniform cool, then you don't have to ask. The only thing you have to decide is whether to wear a skirt or pants. (Just know that before the 70's girls didn't have that choice. It was dresses or skirts.) Now you just have to choose what to wear at home. Your parents may have a say so at home. Mom and Dad may not like it when you're wearing a skirt that's too short or a top that is too low. It's not just because they're afraid that you're growing up too quickly although that is probably true too. They're worried about your safety.

Boys and young men train from birth to be fast with their hands. It's difficult to fight someone tugging on your too short skirt with one hand while pulling at your top with the other. This is where those self-defense classes will come in handy!! (Laugh, it was a joke!)

You're probably thinking "You don't know what you're talking about." Yes, yes I do. I was young once too. Young men and young ladies haven't changed. Clothing styles have changed. Morals have change, but not young people.

It's important to know that what you wear when you walk out the front door is what the rest of the world will judge you by. The first thing most people notice about you besides your eyes or smile is whether or not you respect yourself. Yes, just like what you wear says a lot about you to YOUR friends. It also says a lot to the people around you.

There are two types of parents: one set lets you wear whatever your heart chooses as long as they can afford it, and the other tries to control every piece of their child's wardrobe. Don't despair if you find you have the second set of parents. Why? Because even if your parents don't put down the way you dress, society will. There are unwritten and written words of how people, especially young women and men, dress. Even today.

It's unacceptable to wear sweats to a formal dinner party just like most people won't wear a formal to a ball game. (The second one isn't practical even if your parents own a dry cleaner store). This isn't helping, right? Use common sense. Even if you can afford two closets full of clothes, do you really need it? Probably not!

If you don't have two closets full of clothes, you'll make it. Learn style through accessorizing. You don't have to have a million dollars to look your best.

There's another group of you who don't care about clothing at all. The more choices you have, the easier it is to be confused. Dissatisfied with what you have? It's important to have your own style. It doesn't have to be flashy and show a lot of skin. It doesn't have to cost a lot either. It should never cost you and your family your self-respect and self-esteem. Just remember when you walk out the front door you not only represent you, but your family as well. Life will be better for you if you don't give the rest of the world the wrong message.

It will also be important for you to shower or bathe once a day-of more! There are many great soaps and deodorants on the market. Some are made especially for teens. Experiment until you find one that works for you. Your family may use one type of soap but you prefer another. (Make sure to get all exposed areas and rinse the soap off completely.) Make sure that the one you chose doesn't leave you itchy. If you're unlucky enough to have non-allergy related dry, itchy skin, it's a good idea to find that awesome lotion that makes you feel pretty good when you put it on. The more you like it, the better chance you will put it on. It's also a good idea to stay hydrated and drink at least four glasses of water a day. Six is better ... just keep yourself hydrated.

Shaving ... yes, it's out there now let's talk about it. We all have hair in places we really wish we didn't. (Did I make you giggle?) Under your arms and on your legs are two places you would rather it not be. Be EXTREMELY careful when shaving either. You probably don't want to use shaving cream under your arms because they tend to be extra sensitive. You don't have to use your Dad's shaving cream anymore. They actually make some awesome shaving cream just for us girls. YEAH! Two blades are better than one BUT just make sure you change them out after every fourth or fifth shave especially if you have a lot of hair on your legs. Shave up so when you shave your legs you would go from your ankle to your knees. The same goes for when shaving under your arms. Shave against the grain so to speak. One stroke and rinse. One stroke and rinse. You may have to tap the blade against the side of the tub or sink to get the extra hair off the blade.

How often you shave depends on how fast the hair grows. Some girls will have slow growth and some fast. It all depends on you. If you notice a rash or a pimple type growth, don't shave for several days. The growth is probably an ingrown hair. Make sure to keep it clean and put Neosporin on it. Be sure to change razors often if this happens a lot. BE CAREFUL! It takes a while before you learn your legs well enough not to accidentally "nick" your leg. The blood should stop within seconds. Take your time. NEVER rush shaving. You'll want to wait a few minutes after shaving before applying lotion. Always make sure to rinse your legs well.

For those of you who are unlucky enough to have more hair than usual on your legs, face, arms and more … there are actually new products on the market. Liquids such as

Nair really don't get rid of the hair as efficiently as they claim. This would be a good time to talk to Mom. Let her know that you're worried about your unnatural hair growth. For many years, women (young and old) have used a bleaching process on their upper lip or waxing. This is something else you might want to work out with your mom. Even if she doesn't do this, she will help you.

Eyebrows work with makeup. Eyebrows give expression to your face. What do you want yours to say about you? You can tweeze or wax them as you like just make sure they work with your face. When trying any new product always make sure that it doesn't leave a redness or rash. WARNING! WARNING RAZOR GIRL! When using any new shaving product whether razor or cream and bleaches ... always make sure you don't have excessive redness or rash. If this does happen, you might need to change the type of cream or razor. It's okay to experiment with different types and brands. Just don't give up.

Unwanted hair doesn't have to cause fear and anxiety. We all want to look our best.

No one expects you to look perfect all the time. There might be times when you have to wear sweats in public to the store. But if this isn't your "style" don't make it a habit. In other words, find out what works for you.

Your style, your smile and some awesome attitude will say it loud and proud, "Hello world! I'm here." (I bet you're smiling now.)

Two Ears: All Hearing

Ears ... you've got two of them. They have such a wonderful job. Actually they have several jobs. They help with communication by letting you hear and understand what others are saying. They're really great for listening to awesome music or a loved one saying "I love you".

Ears are used to hold up glasses. There are now hearing aids that are so small they fit neatly into the ear canal where no one can see them. Older forms of hearing aids are large and use the outside flap of ear to keep them in place. You may know people who still have this type of hearing aid. They look clunky, right?

Most people have to make sure not to let the yellowish waxy stuff build up. This will cause hearing loss. Some people actually make too much ear wax. If that's you then your doctor has probably given you medicine for it. Make sure to use it.

Q-tips: you know the little sticks with cotton on both ends. You're not supposed to put anything that small inside your ear canal, but most people put the cotton end inside the ear canal. BE VERY careful if that's what you do.

It's very important to keep all parts of the ears clean. If you have pierced ears or plan on getting them pierced, be sure to clean around the earrings and holes. Even if you've had pierced ears for a while some holes will close up in a year. Others will take ten years to close up.

So the next question might be: what sort of earrings should I wear? These are your accessories. Earrings can be heavy or long. It might be important to pick light weight ones when you first get pierced ears. (Your parents will have to give permission for piercings if you are under eighteen.)

It might be tempting to cover your ears with earrings and holes. Talk to people who've had multiple piercings for at least three years. Why? Because most people who have done multiple piercings within one to two years aren't always going to tell you any problems they might have had with them. After three years, they have an opinion. They'll tell you about any pain or infection worries.

It's without saying that if you take care in how you dress, you will also be careful about picking out your earrings. This is one accessory that won't cost a lot of money, but will leave you feeling pretty awesome! Ears are like eyes, you want to take care of them because without them you'll miss so much.

Don't forget those pearly whites

Twenty-eight (or if you're lucky, thirty-two) pearly whites will be sitting tall and proud in your mouth. The good news is that if you have really great genetics then your teeth will come out perfect. It usually doesn't work that way. "What can I do to help with my teeth to make them pretty?"

Besides going to the dentist for teeth cleanings every six months, you should brush your teeth and use mouthwash at least twice a day. They used to say at least three times a day, but with a busy schedule of school, part-time work or community service and home chores; it might not be possible.

There are other ways to clean off your teeth like rinsing or gargling with water. Gum makers have claimed chewing certain gums will refresh your mouth, but if you think about that idea it won't make sense. It might clean off old foods but it will be sticky on your teeth. (Don't forget to brush your teeth?)

Flossing is also important. Many times when we're brushing our teeth we don't get in the little nooks and crannies between the teeth. This is where dental floss comes in. "But I don't have time to floss?" OR "I don't like the way it feels." Flossing is not most people's favorite things to do when taking care of their teeth. This is why even grownups often chose to not do it BUT it's very important and much easier to do today than thirty years ago.

It's best to do it at least once a day, but if you can do it at least three times a week especially if you have been eating a lot of very chewing foods. It's important to pick the right dental floss for you. They now come in different flavors. There are also toothpicks that have a small piece of dental floss on one end and a pick on the other. Gently slide the string between the teeth and go in a back and forth sawing motion. Do this twice and then pull up. The reason behind only doing this twice is because if you do more, you risk lodging the food back in the hole. You lift up so that it cleanly leaves the tooth area.

When using regular dental floss, pull about six to twelve inches from the container and wrap it securely around your thumb and index fingers of both hands. Of course the back teeth are harder to get to but they still need attention. Don't forget them! Your mouth will feel so clean.

When you have braces, your dentist will explain the best way to take care of them and brush or floss. If s/he forgets, don't be afraid to ask. It's pointless to get braces and then stop taking care of your teeth. If you aren't sure, ask. No one will get angry if you do. In fact they'll be happy to enlighten you.

These are all obvious ways of taking care

of your teeth. There are also some non-obvious ways such as instead of reaching for a soda/cola, reach for a glass of filtered water or bottle of water. Not only will this help you stay hydrated, it will help your stomach and intestines as well as your teeth. The reason behind the filtered water is because at one time scientists believed fluoride helped build strong, healthy teeth. They discovered that an overdose of fluoride has the opposite effect. The teeth actually turn brown and begin to decay.

Water is still a better choice. You need at least six to eight glasses of water a day to stay hydrated. Milk and sunshine help with building strong teeth, bones and hair. Why sunshine? Vitamin D and calcium in milk works better with the UV rays of the sun hitting your smiling face. (Spending a little time in the sunshine even when there's snow outside will help you feel better physically and emotionally.)

What if you don't have perfect teeth? Most people don't. You can brush your teeth three times a day, but sometimes teeth are crooked. There's no answer to why. Now what are you willing to do to take care of your smile? Braces are usually the option of choice. Today braces are a little easier to deal with. They can even be painless.

Braces are still expensive unless your parents have insurance. If they aren't an option while you're a teenager, you're never too old to fix your smile-trust me, I just got braces, and I'm 28! In fact, your body will continue to change until you're twenty-one. If you get braces young, then great. Either way, it's VERY, very important that you take care of your teeth. Not only do people look at them when you smile, you use them to eat with but they help with speech too. When teeth become ill, so will you.

Teeth are like skin. When you get a tooth infection or a severe cut, you're giving germs a way in. A lovely staph or strep infection can set up house and take you down.

Fear of a dentist is normal. It's a super cool if you aren't afraid, but sometimes it's not as simple as most think. If you have a strong gag reflex you may fear choking. Today there are so many dental techniques that can ease your fears.

Don't let the fear of dentists destroy your health. It's important to discuss your fears with your parents and dentist. Take a minute to think about this … don't you want the world to see your dazzling smile?

Welcome to Womanhood!

Welcome to the scary and wonderful world of womanhood! It's a time to celebrate AND a time to mourn. Why? Why should I mourn? I'm happy to walk into womanhood. In some religions and some traditions, the movement into womanhood is a time when you are forced to give up childish ways and begin accepting your entry into womanhood. A hundred years ago this was a sign that you were ready to marry.

Today you're caught between childhood and adulthood. It will seem like nothing has changed except when your period is here. There are so many changes going on inside your body and mind that at times you'll feel like losing it. You aren't alone. You're just learning how to deal with it.

The good news is that every young woman goes through these emotions and feelings. The bad news is that it doesn't stop until, well, if you're lucky … after menopause. What does this mean? It means that on top of having to worry about when you're next period is going to start, you have to deal with your emotional roller coaster. You have choices. This book teaches you how to deal with the ups and downs of life. Your menstrual cycle is one of those life blessings and curses all women deal with.

Maybe you have been dealing with it for a while. Great, then you already know to keep the emergency tampons or pads in your backpack or purse. (If you're lucky you'll get clues that it's coming.) If you start having problems, physically or emotionally, with your period then please talk to someone. Your mom can take you to your doctor if there's a problem.

We all know the basics of the menstrual cycle, but let us go over it anyway. Here's the scientific portion: Most menstrual cycles are twenty-eight days. Normally two weeks before your period your body releases an egg or ovum from your ovaries. If it's not fertilized on its trip down the fallopian tubes then it, as well as the lining of the uterus, is expelled. Voila! You bleed. You can bleed for two days or more. If every time you have a period you bleed for a week or more, run to your Mom NOW! You need to see a doctor. Heavy periods can cause anemia as well as other physical problems. It can also keep you from thinking clearly or even staying awake. This is important.

Talking about your period may not be easy for some of you. Just remember: YOUR mom has been in your shoes. She probably remembers her own fears and frustrations of dealing with her period.

Now let's talk about the large elephant, sanitary pad, in the room. Luckily for you sanitary pads and tampons have become so much more absorbent than in the past. That's the great news. Just like a diaper, don't wait until either is so full that whatever in inside is spilling to the outside. It's also important to mark your calendar. It will help when you go to the doctor. The doctor will want to know the first day of your last period. How long your periods are and how much you bleed. Keep track.

Change the pad every three or four hours. Tampons are different. It you're going to use them, it's important to change it at least every four to six hours. If you need to change it every hour, you might consider using pads. You might have to change to different brands of pads or tampons as some may irritate your skin. The ones without deodorant are actually safer. Don't worry about the smell if you are showering every day. If an odor occurs you need to see a doctor. You have an infection. If you find your pad must be changed two to three times in one hour you should tell Mom immediately. You should see a doctor. Again excessive bleeding doesn't help your health.

The choice to use a tampon or pad is up to you. It's whichever you feel comfortable with. It's very important that during the period that you shower every day. Keep the perineum area clean. (The perineum is the area around the vaginal area and anus.) No, it's not the most fun job you'll ever have but it's important because staph, strep and toxic shock have been associated with tampon usage. (On a side note, it's important to wipe from front to back, always.) You will have to make sure your soap is mild and doesn't irritate your perineum. It's very important that you clean it at least once a day when you shower.

Toxic shock syndrome (TSS) doesn't

happen with every person who uses tampons, but if the young woman or woman neglects herself, she's setting herself up for a possible infection. Toxic shock starts like the flu with a fever and achy feeling and slowly progresses to nausea, vomiting and/or diarrhea. If you feel like you might have TSS tell your mom and get to the doctor IMMEDIATELY.

It's important to take pride in yourself as a woman. It all starts with how you accept your move into womanhood. If you accept it with love and excitement, AWESOME! If you meet womanhood with fear, it will be scary and painful. (There's lots of Tylenol and Ibuprofen to help with the pain.)

Womanhood can be an awesome time in your life. If you're taking care of yourself with positive self-esteem and self-respect, you'll be able to make this journey even easier. You're a young woman now ... **CONGRATULATIONS! You got this!**

It may seem like I gave you so much to think about-which is good thing! Have no fear, it's going to be okay! You are beautiful and you can do anything you have set your mind to. I believe in you! I hope I've encouraged you and made you feel more relaxed. It's all a part of the process-TRUST ME, you are not the only girl this is happening to. You'll be ok. Whenever you need another big sister talk, I'm just an email (askdrciara@gmail.com) away!

Best Wishes,

Dr. Ciara

CPSIA information can be obtained at www.ICGtesting.com
Printed in the USA
LVOW07s2103090816

499677LV00001B/92/P